CW00730213

Rebel Sun

SOPHIE McKEAND

To Dad & Sue,
All my love
now & forever

Sophie x.

PARTHIAN

PARTHIAN

Parthian, Cardigan SA43 1ED www.parthianbooks.com

First published in 2017

© Sophie McKeand 2017

ISBN: 978-1-912109-67-8

Editor: Susie Wild

Cover design by Andy Garside

Typeset by Andy Garside

Printed in EU by Pulsio SARL

Published with the financial support of the Welsh Books Council British Library Cataloguing in Publication Data

A cataloguing record for this book is available from the British Library.

This book is for Rhiannon, Andy, Isaak and our hounds who taught me all about love.

Sophie McKeand is an award-winning poet and the current Young People's Laureate for Wales. Her work has been published widely (*Poetry Wales*, Wales Arts Review, *Dark Mountain, The Lonely Crowd*). She performs regularly across the UK (such as at the Wales Millennium Centre and with *Caught by the River*) as well as internationally (Ireland; the Kolkata Literature Festival, India and Hay Festival, Wales as part of the Valley, City, Village project with the British Council, Wales Arts International and Literature Wales). McKeand has created two hand-stitched poetry pamphlets, *Prophecy: conversations with my Self* and *Hanes*; collaborated on an album, *DRKMTR* (released through the Drum With Our Hands record label); and is the recipient of a Literature Wales Writer's Bursary 2017. She lives in north Wales with her partner Andy and two rescue hounds and can often be found hiking, running, swimming or mountain biking.

www.sophiemckeand.com

 *@SophieMcKeand*

'*Rebel Sun* is a compelling exploration of land and myth, the deep roots of our history, our relationship to nature and to ourselves, merging visions of the past with narratives of the close-up and personal. To hear Sophie McKeand's work aloud is to be captivated, stunned; on the page the poems are no less profound. This is mythological, musical poetry that not only crosses borders but seems to dismantle them entirely, collapsing time and space, transfiguring and prefiguring the world we live in.'

Martha Sprackland

'In *Rebel Sun*, Sophie McKeand is the "peripheral poetess" who takes a grenade to boundaries, dismantles the tight ways poetry is often hemmed-in. This is not experimental work, it is what poetry should be; she takes language to its extreme, challenging the page and the reader with a typography that is as essential as the images that flow and stick with precision. Font, symbol, space, politics, Marxism and Buddhism all interplay. Form unravels content and strands are re-woven; these are breathing, shape-shifting poems, not completed thoughts; image after image drawing the reader closer to understanding about the world at large and in micro, people and spirituality, world politics and the politics of language. She slashes with scissors and weaves with a needle crafted from animal bone. Sophie McKeand has "run barefoot in the language of unfamiliar forests". The *Rebel Sun* translates that experience.'

Clare E. Potter

'A firecracker of a collection. Ideas explode off the page, words pop and fizzle, language and form are ignited and illuminated with the ingenuity of McKeand's searingly bright imagination.'
Kaite O'Reilly

'Sophie McKeand is a force. Her "heart is anchored" in the nature and topography of north Wales. She is intimately engaged with the elements and agents which form landscape. Sophie "speaks hurricanes" and lakes, rain and rocks. In performance and on the page she understands rhythms and controls tides of feelings. Sometimes her images are as sharp and exact as cut slate; other times she glides on experimentation. She has a deep concern for people in danger of alienation and animals threatened with extinction. And she loves lurchers!'
Chris Kinsey

Contents

the disappearing (a manifesto)

Best to be like water,
Which benefits the ten thousand things
And does not contend.
– Lao Tzu

It is time to dissipate
drift like melting ice abandoned
to warming seascapes
days will no longer be carved into the bark
of a life lived immovable.
To spend time tree-like,
rooted
is crucial, a societal debt owed–
      paid in full.
and although we retain the memory
of trees
      we are not trees.

we will follow the seasons
roll with rising suns over land like a herd
of dune horses.

Returning to water, we will pool low
metamorphose with climate
embrace cloudlikelightness–
shape-shift.
We will migrate –
assimilate with murmurations
north for summer
south for winter

and when the mountains call
we will rain.

how they exist

A blind giant of tree-topped heights
lost himself excavating landscapes,
harnessed the strength of ice-choked rivers
–carved oxbow lakes–
flowed into himself (out of himself).

The eyes of a tiny woman who dreamed of trees
were wrenched open by madness,
these images caused her to shrink from people so that
some days she could not bear to exist
and hid inside a nut.

When they met he lifted her onto mountainous shoulders
stood time-steady and guided her eyes to the stars.
In return she folded maps across his body like clouds,
held soft hands over his hollowed eyes.

        They travel as tectonic plates or thunderstorms.

Nothing much settles around them.
The landscape stutters when they move.

Rebel Sun

(i)

Your alarm rings beetles. Opening curtain-heavy eyes you waterfall out of bed. Regrouping in the bathroom you notice manes of dune horses patterning through the window onto new tiles that march like soldiers. Slicing knife-edged blinds across golden plumes, you frown and stand on scales that burp toads – you still haven't lost ten pounds. You try to shower flabby thoughts away but the seal blubber in your mind holds fast and John Lewis doesn't sell the correct excavation knife.

Your car is a tortoise and you grovel to work together. Outside your office the daily protest march has begun. Thousands of bricks defend workers from the insurgent army of brilliant light demonstrating across courtyards. You shield poached eyes from the insurrection and scurry indoors to where strip lights and air-con salve jittery skin. Someone has opened a window near your desk so that you are forced, again, to confront the agitators outside. A swarm of birds occupy plastic trees chanting *comrade! comrade!* to the Rebel Sun.

You decide to take a stand and, lassoing your desk that floats down-office in the flood, type a strongly-worded e-complaint.

You try to sign off with your name but cannot remember. The letters are ants marching determinedly in circles. You brush this diversion aside and type *yours sincerely desk 391*. They will know who you are. You eat lunch at breaktime then buy lunch from the sandwich van parked in tar sands at the back of the building. You are a caterpillar deliberately gnawing through another day. You consider taking up smoking again to curb your appetite.

Some workers are cavorting with birds in the sunlight. They won't last. You've seen it before. Socialising with agitators burns skin to ash. Soon concentration will slosh around the office like over-watered concrete and you will have to dismiss those who are not already blown away by the afternoon hurricane.

You finish work late. There is no traffic. The tortoise is now a hare. Black skies are punctured by bright laser eyes as you surge home exhausted. You are a plague of locusts devouring the contents of the fridge. Blood red wine flows as you settle alone with friends whose scripted conversations intertwine like ivy with social media feeds across the lounge floor. A river of wine finally engulfs the tiny boat in which you are trying to ascend.

(ii)

Saturday screams by in a murder of crows that claw you into Sunday. You intend to spend the day working. The white screen lights a fishbowl around your face as you yank seaweed across the window and submerge. It is cool in the semi-darkness and you breathe into aqua-blue. You could have finished this work on Friday, probably by Thursday; if you're honest, Wednesday, but that's no example to set staff who will loiter like seals at any given opportunity.

The email you are typing refuses to conform, continuing instead to shape the names of places you only know through five-star-all-inclusive-package-holiday-deals. You wonder for a moment about the wider country outside these resorts, maybe next time you'll be more adventurous. You close that screen, cast your net wide, plunge for the depths and begin writing. This is an important document. You know because it arrives as a pulsating jellyfish. You have written these reports a hundred times but it is becoming increasingly difficult to square thoughts. Coming up for air you realise the Rebel Sun has made a tactical manoeuver across the nihilist sky and is streaming into your eyes.

You have no time for distractions and climb onto a chair to block out the mutinous light but the chair is a cockroach and you scream in disgust. Lunging backwards you shatter like a crystal vase across the black slate mountain of the dining room floor.

It is dark. Your eyes are open but filling with thick, black oil. In the corner of the room a white glow beckons. You want to move towards the light but your limbs are shards sunk into coal. Someone will come for you.

It is bright. You are still alone. A mass-lobby of gulls squawks outside in support of the Rebel Sun who parades across your body like a brass band. You try to move away but you are still in pieces. Your laptop is chiming butterflies; your phone rings hedgehogs. It is impossible to reach either. You would sob but that is for feeble people and you are not weak.

(iii)

You lie prostrate before an oppressive sun. The hospital have pieced you together to the best of their ability but insist on rest and recuperation. In sunlight. Your body is a shipwreck. At first you scream every time they weasel you outside but your actions are perceived as a sign of a volatile and unstable character so you acquiesce.

You watch your skin slowly break into dirt and feel your mind crumble. Day after day as the Rebel Sun graffities propaganda across fractured limbs you hold fast to what you know: the sun's malice has caused this depression; you were born to work – to be productive, to give everything to the job, to climb, to improve, to be the best, to be unique, irreplaceable. You hold fast to these thoughts and glare at the sun in the hope he will cower in the face of your defiance but instead you melt into nothingness: you are not special; your employer has already replaced you.

Dissident sparrows squat amongst the shards of your hips and thighs so that you cannot see where you end and they begin. You are pained by the chirrups bouncing around the seashell of your skull and mentally compose their eviction notice.

As the days sloth by a beehive takes shape in your heart. This is totally unacceptable but your complaints go unheard. Time and stillness have gifted you the perception of a hawk and you become engrossed with the actions of certain 'innovator' bees.

At first these tiny entrepreneurs are a mirror in which you vainly admire your own productivity and problem-solving capabilities but, as another afternoon whales past, you realise they are allowing other bees to copy their actions – for free. Not only that but the 'mimic' bees return to the hive to teach other bees the new technique. Each time this happens the hive, and your heart, strengthen and expand but you are aware that the innovator bees hold no leverage, no advantage, and are quickly relegated to being *exactly the same as all the other bees*. You eye them with disgust and begin plotting their removal while surveying the broken remains of your body.

The Rebel Sun has bronzed your skin to dust. Your bones have taken root and are now a hedgerow for sparrows' nests. Your heart is a socialist beehive. Your head is a seashell echoing birdsong. Everything is seasoning by organically. You are no longer needed, or in control. Perhaps this is hell, you muse.

Festival Campsite

We are surrounded.
Our castle-on-wheels
            under siege.

The sun is more – insistent – here – run
now – eat – there – listen – time – to – have – fun.

I have five wardrobes at home
explains the twelve-year-old,
two are double.

I'm reminded of friends saving for kitchens, bathrooms,
decking   and festival time
and what it used to mean.

Watch Tibetan prayer flags:
cerise, mint, snow & aqua whisper
like knickers on a line.
I don't want to tell them no one
is listening

not the geese flying
                V-formation morning
            display
not the

orderly row of poplar trees rolling
like ocean waves –
        like lost pirate cousins.

Instead we learn how to butcher a deer
then drink expensive coffee.

Later we will discuss the price
                    of clothes and art.

Eleven Signs you are Escaping Insanity

A – You accept losing control and imagine floating underwater. As your head emerges you realise this is going to be as difficult or easy as you choose to make it.

B – Blue expanses become inexplicably engrossing as the voluminous azure seeps into your mind.

C – Other people become at once fascinating and a drain. Avoid extensive contact. Their insanity is a religion. Their belief, contagious.

CH – You dream of trees, ache to be surrounded by them and imagine learning through osmosis.

D – *Mae gynnoch chi ymwybyddiaeth mewn amgylchedd. Mae eich mynyddoedd chi'n lonydd.*

DD – You precipitate. Fall to the earth's surface as a condensed form of water.

E – Your awareness expands into new territories. This. Is. A. Good. Thing. Embrace waking dreams, they are a necessary element of your assimilation.

F – The misery of others begins to deeply affect you. You are remembering your humanity.

FF – You soar on the updraft hawk-like – know not-knowing.

G – You finally become aware of the sheer volume of people surrounding you who have lost their minds. The most noticeable sign of insanity is: dull repetitive behaviour.

> G – You finally become aware of the sheer volume of people surrounding you who have lost their minds. The most noticeable sign of insanity is: dulllll repEtiTive behaviOurrr

> > G – You finally become aware of the sheer volume of people surrounding you who have lost their minds. The most noticeable sign of insanity is: duLl repeTiTivve> beeeehavvviouRRrr.

NG – You accept language is defunct and hOwl into reality.

Y Niwl

the forest winters
Y Niwl whispers over
plastic bottles
    swimming slick as
seals through russet
and bracken

year-round-flowering health bar
wrappers flit in flurries
    planted by
walkers and cyclists who gift this litter

to forest spirits
(hang grubby offerings from outspread tree branches)

for thirty kilometres
    or more

minds and bones empty
across landscapes like
watering cans

      but, once unburdened
our explorers

inexplicably find themselves unable to
carry this newfound

                          emptiness home

perhaps it is their eyes overflowing with
                                Y Niwl

        limbs withered with revelations
        of nothing

Elemental

(after Anne Waldman)

I am of you
I am not you
Separate from you
Inextricably linked to you
My heart cannot beat without you

I hear the rain flap wings and fall in love with you
As the sky descends I dream of you
Swim ten thousand miles in you

    Water hold me
    Water know me
    Water wash me clean

You are frozen tundra
I am the fat seal spiralling
The polar bear hunting
The last wandering albatross

You fill the landed depths
I am soft invertebrate (jellyfish, squid)
It is dark, pressure shreds my lungs
I dream of six-gilled sharks

    Water shape me
    Water form me
    Water fill my needs

You are grey slate
The weighty unknown

I am vessel-shaped
I am broken pottery
I shape-shift
I am sand, granular
I dessicate
I sing for clouds
I sing to the sky
and wait and wait
(Water is time)

       Water erase me
       Water expunge me
       Water fill my dreams

I was skulls buried deep
I was excavation
I was twenty elephants beheaded
I was the poacher
I was the gun
I was the thick rasping saw hacking through
grey skin that parted like the Red Sea
I was men marching to war
I was men hunting wolves
I was men exploding mountains
I was men razing forests
I was women raped
I was crime-scene-activity
I was electric-shock-therapy

I was the knife at your neck
The bullet in you back
I was Nazi salutes at dawn

Water remember me
Water forgive me
Water help me redeem

You are mercurial
Blue gliding
Blue tumbling
Blue engulfing
Patch-worked blue fields and blue leopard-mountains

I am woman
I am all of the women
I hold you
fold you into myself
I count time
I count stars
My skin wrinkles like tissue paper
I age and learn to not know
I grow tree-like, gnarled
Bark is my art
Split stripped and silvered
I branch
My roots search for you
Tear down buildings to reach you
Braid across roads to drink you
Suffocate boulders to touch you

Water know me
Water love me
Water wash this world clean

Cosmic Sat Nav

I want the money I give my life over for
To mean something, he said
which was the final step – or the first.

Packing two lives and two dogs
into 2940mm x 1193mm x 7340mm
requires planning.
We are not leaving home –
we are taking home with us
with nothing to let go of we hold
onto what is precious
and keep filling each other's gaps.

I believe him.

Skin contours like littered
retirement maps
(too young to wait to die – old enough to

      break   from these railway
                              lines:

flick switch on the cosmic Sat Nav
repattern our lives to unwind across the land like ivy
run barefoot in the language of unfamiliar forests
swim in an orange sun.

      There is nothing to escape
      when embracing the wind.

Cymro

Brother, I have challenged you. Tundra flesh and frozen hearted, I watched your struggles. The ice wind blowing from north to south, east to west, I exhaled sleet and thunder, manifest lightning and war.

Brother, I was indifferent to you. The hard slate of argument and self-righteous rock of years – compressed memories, pain and hurt. Strata of misunderstandings and the knowledge that 'I' am always right (we dig the richest seams).

Brother, I have hated you. Wished you in heaven, and hell. Felt skin itch quick and prickled at your actions. Experienced scorched words launched hot, so I returned, always returned, quick-fire molten rocks.

Brother, I have wept for you. When the wasteland between us, became us, and the barren earth we ravaged crippled us (founding fathers) so that the bare trees shuddered at our thoughts and wild rivers rusted at our words and black crows spiralled from the sky where we trod.

Brother, I stand before you. Mouth of ash and dust, eyes of mirrors, glass shattered at the carnage created by men who would tear this land apart just to be *right*.

Brother, I kneel before you. I never believed in fate, or our ability to wound each other, I only dreamed of what was rightfully mine and did not want you to have the capacity to love, or sow seeds, plant crops, gather fruits, sit under wide oak trees and laugh in sunlight, without me.

Brother, I hold my arms out to you. Because our future can only flourish when people of every origin rooted here, grow together. Cymru is *our* country – land of brothers, a family of all races and none, and soon the mountains in which we forge incandescent songs will echo with our children's bright voices.

Brother, I will carry you. For as long as it takes. For as far as it takes, I will shoulder your story because it is also mine and we will sow poetry across these Welsh mountains and valleys together. We are the untameable forest. The hard slate. The mighty seas. The rolling skies.

The strength of our community, the artistry of our words will galvanise hearts across this troubled world so that the legend of the brothers of Cymru is celebrated long after we have

folded into earth.

07:31 to Cardiff

The train was late this morning

Which is good

Because I was also late

Pounding the pavement from home to station

With a twilight-filled head

And a pocket of Facebooks

I watch the sky lower a grey ceiling

(Journey south with strangers)

And live the phrase under the weather.

The day is spent sharing experiences like biscuits

With creatives. I am grateful for their

Friendship. And the work.

But the train tracks are unravelling

M y i n t e s t i n e s —

Threading them out across landscapes —

A thin membrane of webs

Spinning through time, a debt to the weaver

increases with each trip as I snatch at tenuous

Connections – only   ever a minute. to   s p a r e

Fair Trade

Shell shocked –
the squish of soil and life beneath feet exchanged
for the dead pad of carpet and
I am bereft.
The exhaustion of returning to a house
Is a giant sucking the marrow from bones.

This is not Fair Trade:
Mortgage
Life insurance
Pension
Sick pay
Holiday pay
Security

                    For freedom

Four words run on loop in the mind:

            All. Ownership. Is. Theft.

And I realise that to die with nothing
        will mean we have truly lived.

Declutter

Eighteen pairs of shoes including one with a heel completely missing two needing heel studs three pairs so vertiginous I am in pain if wearing them for more than an hour at a time and only put them on if we go out for meals six pairs of flat pumps three of which are nearly identical fourteen dresses three black two plum two pale blue halter-necks that haven't suited me in years two white netting petticoats plus an electric blue one that looks fabulous but I only wear twice a year twenty-two pairs of socks twenty-five pairs of knickers eleven handbags four of which are broken and I haven't bothered to fix nine shirts five of which don't fit properly seven bras with underwire and padding I've stopped wearing when did I believe the lie that my breasts are so horribly deformed I should only subject the general public to them when they're lifted with wire and hidden behind a layer of moulded foam six sets of pyjamas some of which are torn eight pairs of jeans three blue three black and two in colours I don't like three pairs of cropped trousers ten skirts some fifties some secretarial-tube-style that are quite uncomfortable so I can't be bothered wearing them eleven lipsticks no twelve lipsticks half of which I hate three mascaras two need throwing out various wide fitting elastic belts skinny belts in silver and blue that don't go with anything brown belts that look ugly and cheap one red duffle coat that was my daughter's two wool trench coats one from Oxfam one from the Heart Foundation in town one waterproof walking coat one cagoule twenty-plus scarves I don't even wear scarves anymore except the ones on my head which makes another four I bought some others from eBay but they're too shiny and slide off my head not such a great deal when I never wear them endless hair grips and bands I don't like an entire box of jewellery I don't wear I don't wear any jewellery T-shirts in every colour I don't wear except instead of the pyjamas that I also don't wear piles of books some that I have never read some I have started reading and hated but didn't want to admit I thought they were pretentious or just fucking boring other books that mean so much to me I ignore them on a daily basis but knowing they are there is a comfort books I used to love that I can't read now but can't bear to give away because I used to love them books the dog has chewed but I can't bring myself to throw away books with misleading titles that I've immediately regretted buying online Terry Pratchett books with yellowing pages older than my daughter and I've moved on from them but he taught me so much Agatha Christie books which were the first to genuinely shock me so that I can still remember the jolt when the culprit was finally revealed in Murder Is Easy but that I haven't read in over twenty-five years the entire Harry Potter series because I read them with my daughter and remember the point at which she became independent and would make me wait until she'd read them so I'd read up to her page once she'd gone to bed so we could talk about it in the morning endless endless poetry books that are still not enough poetry books I have so many to read it is too much I cannot read all the poetry books three bikes an Orange Five Diva Pro with full suspension bought over two years on interest free credit a French shopper gifted from my dad a road bike for triathlons which cost a hundred quid from eBay but I only did three races and the first two were on my old hardtail that I did eventually sell to buy this one because four bikes is too many although I've regretted selling it every day since what if I want to go on a ride that doesn't need full suspension but a bit of off roading might happen a mountain of sports gear for running riding and swimming at least half of which I don't wear because it's too loose or too tight or has malfunctioned in some way or that just makes me look fat half open jars of jam and chutney and homemade cranberry jelly I only make at Christmas that never gets finished enough plates and cutlery to invite the whole street round for dinner as long as they don't mind the mismatched dinner service not that I ever invite them around we're so busy with work and life we don't even see our own families enough or our long-term friends we did invite our Polish neighbours around once but it's becoming awkward because they're really hospitable and keep inviting us back and now we've been there nearly ten times while they've only been here that one time I think we might have to start avoiding them soon they are so lovely and a constant reminder of our neighbourly failings and then there are the letters Dear Ms McKeand we regret to inform you that on this occasion your application has been unsuccessful Dear Ms McKeand your water bill is now overdue Dear Ms McKeand you are eligible for our new low credit card rate of just 6.9% on balance transfers and we have after careful consideration increased your limit to £7,500 Dear Ms McKeand thank you for your recent submission unfortunately Dear Ms McKeand your tax returns are now overdue Dear Ms McKeand we are delighted to accept your work and that of course is the diamond in the pile of crap that makes it all worthwhile but why I keep them all is beyond me why I keep any of it is the question although perhaps I worry that once I start decluttering I won't know where to **stop.**

Minimalist Living

delete

anything   that

is   not
needed

ask

only
what
is

essential

then

halve

gestation

I woke one morning with
something growing inside me
                no – that is not true

nothing was inside me
                then something but
                         I did not know
                                        for some time

                    perhaps a few hours, or a day, or a year,

                but she was there
                      & I was sick

                  she became
                      & I was t i r e d

this newness weaving into me
                was exhausting

&ISLEPT&SLEPT < it was a. difficult. time. >

        on reflection I would have done everything differently
        (or changed nothing)
but it is only through doing
that we learn to not do

& I cradled her } refused to send her out into the world
for some long time

     now she is one of many
        lounging around the mind
I teach them to cope with rejection
     by sending them back out into the world

by stepping out of myself

    by planting stones

Waiting for Awen

At the station you stand and watch for *Awen*.
A tannoy announces she is late (or you are early).
Snowflake manuscripts are cradled onto slush piles
by the hot air of mouths –
dissolve into warm piss and
criticism.

You wait where the tracks are well-worn as the next
three trains enter and exit
each one stuffed like a writer's bookshelf
each one whispering: *Awen-Awen*
                              Awen-Awen

You are on the wrong platform, a moon-face
states eyeing the texts wrapped around your frame.
You shrug. Their eyes are cameras. You are a smear across the
lens.

Another train departs. Another *missed opportunity*.
Another moon face – perhaps *you don't want it enough*.

A childhood line crystallises in the fog:
I want doesn't get. You exit the station.

Outside, blowing alphabets onto cold fingers, you scramble
over the bones
of a winter afternoon; poke fingers into eye sockets of dead
poets for leverage.

Halfway up and exhausted you twist to witness the people
stacked on trains and
shiver to imagine how far ahead they are by now: *Awen-Awen*
                                                          Awen-Awen

Reaching the summit, frosted mulch crunches
as you crawl. Your hands are badger's paws foraging through
the ice-crusted
    earth of your ribcage for
        a seed.
Deeper you rummage, snapping rib and root
until your elongated weasel nose unearths an acorn:
one. seed. of. truth.

The ritual begins.
The ground cleared.
            The acorn planted.

        You wake with roots for lungs.
You will cough earth and lies for ten years   and with
        each aspiration whisper:

                        Awen   *Awen*
                Awen   *Awen*

Community Artistry

I have given
your name
to roots &&
pioneers
 (I am mycorrhizal fungi)

| you are birch | you are rowan |

you are not alone
        (do not run)
your legs ramble & will tire
teeth   chatter
        { clipping streams }

or seal-swimming with piranhas
¿sut dach chi'n gweu efo'ch gilydd?

art – is – squabbling gulls
{when the knitting is complete   no one remarks on the needles}

I am the poem proclaiming love for you
cat-er-waul-ing-at-mirr-rrors
                in dreams we are moth-light
                                shoulder your tears
                                mouth over hot coals
                                absorb fifty gallons of water
                                & cradle the flood

– prejudices-wound-ivy-taut – we knit frothed waves –
   snuggle tiny children onto bright beaches
    && count creatively &&
    ¿how many breathed water today?

we will tie knots of remembrance
  solder golden fractures through our
grandmothers' bowls
  //drink their stories by stolen milklight//

the wise sew our future with buttons |
      chant the neighbours' tongues:

Croeso: Welcome: سهلا و أهلاً : Welkom: Bienvenue:
Willkommen: *K α λ ῶς O ρ ί σ α τ ε* : Hoş geldiniz:
स्वागत: Céad míle fáilte: Witamy: *Добро пожаловать!* :

  – the trees are invading our minds –
      & these last words
        we scatter

Sale

Ladies and gentlemen we've reached our final lot for the evening with a most exquisite piece. I see our discerning audience are eager to commence bidding (a beauty like this is rarely seen at auction) so I'm delighted to present: one timeless, floor-length coat cut to a stunning neoliberal economic pattern guaranteed to smarten the most discourteous dictatorship or hold a smart slimline shape around the flabbiest socialist derrière.

Note the elegantly tailored lapel and lavish diamond pin cut-and-crafted in Israel from Zimbabwean stones. The ethically minded (and who isn't these days?) will be delighted to learn the internationally recognised Kimberly Process approves these diamonds as conflict free. Ownership of this pin alone places you within an extremely select clientele of African and Middle Eastern royalty as well as A-List celebrity.

During its impressive life this garment has accrued some interesting characteristics and a number of you have, quite rightly, expressed concern at recent repairs and relatively new designs migrating up from the hem and in from the sleeve. We have slowed these refashioning attempts by encouraging newcomers to shape their attire from cloth in our earlier auctions. Unfortunately, with a coat this unique, we have been unable to devise a method of unpicking the errant stitching that does not corrupt the extraordinary nature of the piece as a whole.

The highly sought-after black-rhino-horn-buttons are expertly sourced and crafted to hold against the most challenging insurgencies, while the fur lining, generously donated by an Arctic Fox no less, cocoons the wearer against the forecast freezing storms. You will be snug with the knowledge that purchasing this coat supports China's burgeoning fur trade, lifting thousands of peasants out of poverty and into decent, honest livelihoods.

It is important to note great care must be taken when attempting to clean this garment as certain ethnic threads (unintentionally incorporated at the point of creation) may unravel and, although this might not initially appear to be an issue, experience has proven the coat will disintegrate if subjected to excessively high levels of sanitisation.

A Victorian-style-blouse is recommended to complete this sensational outfit: *ruffles are this season's hottest accoutrement.*

Seller's note: tax breaks and additional subsidies are available.

our histories have deserted us

-our-stor-ies-are-blown-to-the-wind-like-sand-

(everything issss in A
cOnnn//sT?anT st))Ateee ovv
moOvem...e&nt)

!
watch
people battle
to save
castle-high
sand dunes being
gobbled by sea waves
gnawed by HIGH TIDES
We. Must. Save. The. Sand!

but elsewhere   sand begins
-blowtrickling-
fingering   under doorways
banking against walls
banking against walls
&& our army of cleaners
fight to
STOP
the tide of t i n y g r a i n s
this relentless creation of

A.N.
Other
sand dune

collector of songs

we will give the people songs of hope
X-factored [*yn Saesneg*]

¡swelling & welling eyes!
¡hearts & hopes!
¡&welling & swelling!

> *this is what you've waited for for 12 years*
> *this is what turning into a star feels like*

we watched him implOde

a billion bits lit TV screens
eclipse the sun
then   blOwOut

we had to change the fuse twice
before police answered our
999 emergency calls

too late to save
our daughters   scarred   with

                                    his name

expectation
neu addo a bygwth

two were cooking
juice knifed through
red & her death
like winter
eat this he said delirious

it threatens rain tomorrow
& I breathe
rubble knowing

     it will be better for hardworking families
       because this is 'change that will make a difference'
as opposed to change that's really the same
or 'unchange'
as the pragmatist understands it.

we fashion our bones to shackles
so as not to be feckless scroungers:
              old
           disabled
            young
              ill

clouds distend heads
\feel them bloat behind eyes\

     bydd hi'n ddiwrnod ansefydlog yfory gwasgedd isel
     yn dod â gwyntoedd cryfion a glaw}}}

we gorge on larder rats
their bones gifted & wrapped

city 'scape

lights felted
in winter rain
it's pelting
down our skins thrum
the sound of
our mouths closing

mouths closing like windows
protesting the
unwashed tides
threatening to wring
our roots
from *our* earth

our earth we shit
on like pigeons
we hate their
highly corrosive faeces
<the relationship is
anything but amicable>

but amicable like rats
weaving tales of
'too many passengers//
who built this nation?'
they did without permission
& our gold

our gold stolen from
their great-great-
grandparents | giftwrapping
ourselves in
smog-like-civility we
hope they choke

first

swansong

Anarchy must never happen
I could punch a swan in the throat tomorrow
     then where would we be?

with Rioja-fuelled freedom
we pen lakes
and sing!

    if you approach a swan's nest on the river she might get aggressive
    an hiss an flap wings, but the danger's over-rated an it's a myth
    she'll break yer leg or arm with
    her w i n g s

it's said the swan drowned a man
    white snow
    white death
    white noise

he should've learned to swim

not gannet liquid
        in hindsight the punch was a mistake.

If we'd kept him | under control | tighter control |
but the anarchists demanded
the right to punch a swan

and we must live with the
consequences.

Paper News

I am panic
I am the tearing
I am nightmarish scenes greeting police
I am sickened
I am reviled
I am dismay

I am flood warning
I am winter warning
I am stay indoors warning
I am severe weather warning
I am hurricane force winds warning
I am droughts to hit the south of England warning
I am hosepipe bans
I am swimming bans
I am hotter than anticipated
I am deserts forming
I am 50 degrees c in the Middle East
    and they're all going to have to move somewhere – warning

I am paper
I am the test paper
I am litmus paper

    Light the paper
    Spark the fuse

I am justifications for war in Iraq

I am drones dropping bombs on schools in Syria
I am the only hospital for 50 miles decimated
I am collateral damage
I am screaming for my sister
I am screaming for my brother
I am burying my family
I ululate for my family
I am the freedom fighter
I am the terrorist
I am Muslim
I am Islam
I am ISIL
I am fear
I am your eyes
I am your ears
I am the hot salt of blood and ash
I am coming for you
I am coming for you
I am coming for you

I am armies of migrant families invading your communities
I am the soft bodies of refugee children washed onto your shores
I am critical scenes at Dover and Calais
I am young migrant men hijacking lorries
I am children trafficked
I am mothers raped
I am not sorry (it is not our fault)
I am telling you to send them back
I am go home or face prosecution
I am impartial
I am impervious

I am swarms
I am cockroaches
I build barricades
I burn camps
I tear down shelter

I am paper
I am the test paper
I am litmus paper

     Light the paper
     Spark the fuse

I am young black man arrested
I am more young black men shot by police
I am Black Lives Matter
I matter
I am All Lives Matter
I matter
I am unbiased
I am white
I am privileged
I am male
I am single-white-female

I am *papier-mâché*
     Stripped and moulded into
                terror

I am gunshots ringing across the playground
I am gunshots fired at police

I am gunshots in the busy shopping mall
I am lone wolf male
I am disturbed white male
I act alone
I speak for no one

I am paper
I am the test paper
I am litmus paper

    Light the paper
    Spark the fuse

I speak for you
I speak for your fears
I speak so you don't have to
I tell it like it is
I tell your fortune
I am your problems solved
I am the voice of your wife
I justify your fantasy
I am lap dancers earning ten grand a month
I am sex workers who. love. it.
I am prostitution
I am money
I am the money you want to spend
I am the hours you need to work to matter
I am the crippled NHS
      and we all know whose fault that is
I am sick people fiddling benefits
I am the poor who could get a job if they bothered

I am single mothers shelling out babies for your taxes
I am warden
I am judge
I am critic

I am tissue paper for your tears
I am tissue paper for your fantasies
I speak for you
I speak your mind
I am your friend
I am transparent
I am impartial
I am information
I am sensational headlines
I am no editorial bias
I am right-wing-think-tank-expert-opinion
I am the future
I am your present
I write your past
I am right (there is no left)

I am paper trails
I am words
I am the universe in pages
I am your world
I am your friend
I am paper-thin
I am paper news
I am newspaper

Light the paper
Spark the fuse.

Silver Fish

For months Trump spattered fish as he spoke,
bright flashes of silver battered windows while we fought
friends for wheelbarrows and shovels.
With arms like nets we trawled neighbourhoods, snatched
riches from each other: stockpiled cod, mackerel
and sturgeon on porches;
boxed shoals into Great American Lounges.

Now the deluge has ended we whale
guard-with-guns our mountains of silver
our children's future
slowly being poached by a Rebel Sun.

Process
(in memory)

process & form & forms & commmuni-cat–ionnn

I have slept four-hundred-and-thirty-nine times since
I do not remember

synaptic sTutter // something was All overrr thenews
    roedd o'n dydd Iau yn Gymru

[if I ever hurt you please forgive me]

she said — 'I find the *action* in my body'
I search my body for memory
        I have no action | I do not remember

a white boat twists its blue   bilge skyward
& the command (I love you)
        'stay there'
//not processed by the one-hundred-and-seventy-two//
survivors//
rescued InFishIngBoatS

            —-you evade

<<I have slept four-hundred-and-thirty-nine times since>>
I do not remember

& search for the action in my body
    capSize

'there are a few people in the ship
we are not dead yet'
CapsiZe

pin yellow ribbons
I think we're really going to die
I search my body for this memory:

*it was eight fifty-eight on Thursday sixteenth of April two-
thousand-and-fourteen the sky was grey the sun wrapped in cloud
I just jumped into the water and started swimming it was really
cold so I tried to swim as fast as I could*

'가만히 있으라'

lifeboats suck the boat like barnacles
white shelled & static
//not for the three-hundred-and-four who died//
some were rescued InFishIngBoatS

—you evade

   processing grief
I search for this action in my body
pin yellow ribbons
it was eight fifty-eight on Thursday sixteenth April two-
thousand-and-fourteen
the water was frigid
nearly three-hundred pupils and their teachers remain missing

tilt ten degrees/shift/tilt ten degree meme   me   me-me
       memory
three hundred and four people die

I had a dream of swimming in the sea all week:

바다 속에서 헤엄치는 꿈을 일주일 내내 꾸었습니다

this is the process by which we remember

we are OverlOaded:
nine-hundred-and
-seventy-eight tonnes of grief

two thousand tonnes of tears are needed to ballast | to balance
                                —and still you evade

synaptic sTutTer//process & form
she was in no state to carry passengers

topography (*plygu*)

| *mewnblyg* |
I fold at the reservoir
slate surfaced
-creased—froth-

in the time before Understanding I
lived through ice age & flood
was desert &
rock
the Great Beginning tattooed on bark & flesh
(I am not the woman I was)

      terra nullius

    cartographer's
breadthless
lengths
caress
    soles
//held hostage to shadow & son//

mynyddoedd
{ f o l d - o u t }
   | *allblyg*
      the wall cracks |

      I whisper I love you

conservation

in one year Namibia was the site of almost 16,000 trophy hunts
but the real figure is probably much higher

        we are conserving life
I was so honoured and blessed to be a part of your life during
my hunt. You welcomed me with such warmth and hospitality

the big cat was skinned and had his head removed
(amber marbles replace eyes)

I knew this was coming, yet I couldn't help but to feel
overwhelmed
                          am I hooked on hunting?
                          you better believe I am

we keep the windows open as pressure from explosions can cause
glass to break this is one of the lessons we've learned from war

      I was shot with an arrow, stalked for 40 hours, then killed
        with a rifle that weighed no more than a newborn baby

the kills increase: 140,000 | 210,060 | 220,000

        so that we might conserve life

over 600 detainees and political prisoners die under torture:
    killing in fenced-off private property is easier than gunning
                        them down on their own turf

a trophy to be proud of
I know my rights as a human being

I wanted a quality hunt but not one that would break
the bank since I've worked hard all my life
to save for my hunt
this is one of the lessons we've learned from war

I cannot put into words what this hunt
means to me
April 14th – the quiet mornings are over the horrible
shelling sounds and smoke clouds are back

my father and brothers were murdered
but the real cost is probably much higher
he was skinned and had his head removed

I know my rights as a human being

the Predator
has been modified and upgraded to fire two AGM-114
Hellfire missiles

I knew this was coming,
yet I couldn't help but to feel overwhelmed

I wanted a quality hunt but not one that would break the
bank since I've worked hard all my life to save for my hunt

our streets are shattered
we must evacuate

the kills increase: at least 320,000 casualties – over half of
them civilian

    but the real figure is probably much higher

       Am I hooked on hunting? You better believe I am
these are the lessons we learn from war

    this is the conservation of life

Inside Goldstein's Mind

i. red
"In a letter he wrote:
*At seventeen I was red through and through, though I didn't
know Marx from a matzo ball.*"*

At this time

Goldstein 4 is not   catalogued

you follow red:

The Marx-Engles Reader

Marx and the Trade Unions
Capitalist Production as a Whole by Karl Marx

you crouch in the construction   sited

the air is tight

mind-as-machine   crunches
conception concrete composition

'the crises are always

but momentary'

[bookmarked by *Russian Literature Week*]

on rubble strewn
bedrock structures
are staked & shaped
search for posts &
marks the words
are not hidden he
planted where the
ground is fertile.
you water and wait.

ii. ten rooms

ten rooms disintegrate

the mind

dissolves across catalogues

you walk to

Goldstein 9 (100)

the corridor

lights

automaton, blind closed to

141.4 *The Discovery of the*

Individual

you decide to

begin at Goldstein 7

(400, 500, 600, 700) stride

the horseshoe &

immerse in

Japanische Tuschmalereien

where characters rain

from doubled pages

studied

landschaft air evaporates

cognition Leonard

speaks it does not

matter who you

are you leap

mountain ridges – together

arrive at

Boring Postcards USA

iii. the connector

I spend time with Goldstein's imagination –
    gossamer pages veined with theories & syntax
annexed to over 13,000 books
    cocooned by a mind secreting threads
     that span continents –
spinning connections between worlds
with opinions more resolute than
    high-grade steel, more durable & elastic
    than the strongest man-made fibre

     he extends Marxist theory

to students ballooning

      away

        on the breeze.

The Problem with Young People

Are you hurting?
You can't be that upset
Your hurting isn't really hurting
You're too young to really hurt
You'll get over it
I did when I was your age

It's not real pain when you're young
You   bounce
You live
You have everything to live for
Shrug it off
Move on
Time heals everything (everything)
You'll be fine

What about me? (What About Me?)
Why should you get all the attention?
It is as hard for me
Working for no thanks
Drinking to numb the stress
My husband has diabetes and heart trouble
Who cares about him?

We all suffer
Nobody helped me
I had to just get on with it
I have to just get on with this   life

You'll have to just get on with it, like I do
Didn't do me any harm
No harm at all

The problem with young people these days
Is they think the future is all about them
Well, nothing comes for free (for free)

I can't begin to tell you
How hard it's been
For me.

disarmament

I fucking hate poetry
is not a great start

but also not the worst
that's okay I didn't like poetry

in school and smile through liquid morning air
at gate-faced indifference. Tell me something

about you *there's nothing to tell I don't*
do nothing don't go nowhere

the imagination's a battlefield
ransacked by years

of fire-sales and marching-state-orders
we circle blank slate camouflaging

image and feeling. I drop the pen, reach
down throat past scars,

anxiety and the fear I'm terrible
at this. Cold fingers snag a white

flag I haul the poem from open mouth
watch their eyes watching.

Flo

the river courses backwards
sometimes   pools and Eddie's
forgotten to meet her

      again
we've been sat here all day trying to work out this damn
diary it's the days you see — they don't make sense

                          moments riot in winter squalls
                                  falling into
                          memories | reflecting
               across a thousand bright rain bubbles that
                                pop surface then

      echo downstream
           eCHhooOo Ddowns:tream
      e>c,,H/o,d)wNstre___am

I'll paddle here just in
case he comes — did he say what time he was coming?

      she is water & time
      (reshaping landscapes)
         mother & wife
      storyteller & birdsong

rainstorms dismantle bridges like Lego
uproot yesterdays like saplings
biography dissolves
into
sinkholes

and in the clear stream of her cerulean eyes
the grey heron waits

migrating nowhere

How. To. Ask. For. Help.

        drown near someone with a rope
                            or rafffft
                                orr a dIInghhy
this is only helpful
                    ifyouknow
                            what a
dIInghhy   is
and what it can do for you
          ¿what can it do for you?

*during our first visit we discovered the villagers had nothing and
yet did not seem to recognise how impoverished they were so we gave
them everything we had and upon returning were greeted with faces
begging us for help 'look how poor we are' they mouthed this is*

How. To. Create. Poverty.

                   ¿¿can yOuu ??heL.>>p m.e/e??

I (the drowning woman) might say – 'my,
                    that's a   strong rope'
                    perhaps you might agree thank you
orr I might say that rope might be a
      wonderful life
           line for somebody.
.you nod.
                    ¿is one still drowning?
¿AM I STILL DROWNING?

let's tAke anothheer example:
I leave myself open because I do not trust you and when you
take what is not yours (which eventually you will) my mistrust
will be validated

{she is very open}

or maybe I don't ask for the rope
or rafffft or dIIInghyyy
because I need to learn
to swim which is a moot point
.I am a strong swimmer.
I could exit the water
.this.is.not.drowning.
I was never drowning.
the rope is a lie.

I am the Ocean.

hope//less

I am giving my hope to you / hold it well / keep it safe and do not / lose the path / I cannot carry this burden / it is too great / and I am tired // the light fades / I see you already / shoulder the hopes of others & worry / you will sink into the dark night // / / :; Ii waatch y0oou sinkk intotthe darknight.

Reincarnation
(or the visualisation of patriarchy)

After he sucks out the brain
he tosses her skull
into a fire of lizards.

Each orange reptile vaults further
than the last, scrambling for the darkness
away from the fire and moon-rocks
that throttle it.

Like embers, they soon begin
to blacken and die, dissolving into earth
with a slight groan (as if the man were
                                        making love) before
        reincarnating in the fire.

As each skull fractures against the rocks
        a starling
materialises in the gilded cage of his chest

on and on this macabre scene unfolds:
he opens the cage door,
reaches in to snag a bird with his ham-fist,
examines her for a moment then
wrings her neck, bites off her head and
hurls her body onto the mountain.

cumulonimbus

When the elite men of the world had finished lecturing,
(their last tombstone marked heavy upon the map of the earth's
gossamer wings) she flapped once causing

                myriad cities of reason to fold; an atlas of
concrete slabs to crumple into soil, and vast tenets of intellect
to be spewed at an indifferent sky.

The Rebel Sun melted the swords these great men had refused
to fall upon (the staunchly defended coastline of their honour
long eroded by relentless waves of criticism)

  with no one to tell them how to think the people
dispersed like ghosts.

    Groping for meaning in the half-life they
          eventually congregated as massive cloud formations:

      cirrus | altostratus | cumulonimbus | stratocumulus

in this form they heard only the voice of mountains
                            tumbled as rain from
cerulean skies in praise of slopes and crevices and ridges

and

finally understood what it is to be
in the presence
of greatness.

InsOmnia

The monster under my bed fears the line above it
The line above my bed fears the monster below it
Whisper work experienced work whisper
Metaphorically speak-innnngng I sleep in a bunk
(romance is bed—dead)

P-p-p-peripheral-p-ppoetssss
Problems with repose-inning/written poorly
Perfectly pieced people reposed less
&& personify insomniaccc-ic-cal irrelations
Orrrr orgasMm.
What rhyming nonsense hate is. Mate.
My boreful daemons wax lyrical
Dance beautiful in the liminal grey of
Sleeplessnesses of dreamless-distressesess
Of nighttime obsessions && lies (he cries/she cries/we cry/
they all fucking cry)
Not a dry eye eyed implies prideless (disguised with asides)

Orrrrrrrganise yourrrr serious words//sleep with them
Nightly poignant && thoughtless
Lessened by the writer before me
Frank thoughts sublime-inal//what is baddder than gooder??
More shitter than selfreferentialselffself edit. ed.it. E.dit.ed.
<<definitely how to do not it not how do definitely to it do
not>>
Bitter anger {orange-coloured barometer} franking time
sublime time time is sublime time timed nightly

Efforts ::footinarse:: distorted words of inverted praised efforts
Relational relay remarks remade innnn insomniacical
indifference

I CNT GO ONNN!!
Bulli-mic vomiting of language
Pass the bowl!
Pass the bile!
Mock mock flock letters docked apologies pocked
Squawk completely sorry squawk sorry completed meme
sorreeeeee

&& finally dawns the death of sense
I weep! Did You sleep?
My deep heart shuns irony
(Poetically speaking – to the light! First light!)

I ask one more time – *did you sleep last night?*

My Mother Speaks Thorns

Twisting dense & sharp
from open mouth
her words become sparring Red Kites
that maul our secrets.

After they have shredded my guts across the lawn
she collects me back up,
fashions bright innards
into bunting,
ties them to a tree to
fight the wind.

When the birds are sleeping
she will call me to swim with her
in a dark lake edged with silver moss.

But I am wiser now
with bones of coiled snakes,
thorns of my own
and I cannot swim
for the tangle of our hair.

Iron Will

My father wears iron shoes
flattens the earth under his broad feet.
He remains unrusting,
with a flat moral certitude
and a love of doing things correctly.

Walking slowly, deliberately
straight as rail tracks
he blasts tunnels through mountains
so as not to deviate.

– His slow rhythm commands
this way – this way – this way
do not question. Head north.
His compass could take him to the moon

but the shoes keep him grounded
slogging on through clay & bog
along riverbed & creek
his iron-clad feet beat
the ground, one step, one step

with the weight of the world.

Bearhug

My sister pushes the points of sharp bear nails under
my diaphragm, shovels downward until white seagulls explode
from my stomach with the sound of shrieking children.
She digs inside – furred arms slick to elbows,
rummaging for the wrong I've done.

I tell her she is a warrior
feared guardian spirit
Berserker

but she is focused on the hunt for skeletons
– her paws grip my heart and I slap her hard
across the face.

I whisper that she is a powerful symbol carved on totem poles.

She slows, listening, tiring,
it is cold now and she has gnawed over every bone.

Her paws excavate a large den on the steep,
north-facing slope of my ribcage.

She clambers in to hibernate.

I am winter-frost, insulating her dreams
with a thick blanket of snow.

follow the white dog

she carries your heart in her mouth
do not lose her
– beat – quick –
trot expansive streets
      and check your tears

you will travel over a decade
(and not depart)

she tracks hedgerows that haunt you
      is cherry blossom blown across
           soot-smeared windows
you are fractured rib & branch devoted
to a city mirroring
      the wilderness that dreams you

dim light shatters with each
              stride

    she hunts

    with your heart in her mouth
    with your heart
    with you

follow the white dog

downhill

my name is Sophie
it's been eight months/four weeks – no — twO dAys
since my last {ride}

it's raining
in Cymraeg: *mae'n bwrw glaw*
Bwrw (boo-roo): to hit, to rain, to imagine:
I imagine a map

we are not lost
this is a>>detour>>>
&claw up through knee-deep rusted mulch
27 lb of bike hiked onto back && it's still raining
three hours from the car in any direction
tyre-grip greased rock
| rear mech | clicks mouth | floods in |
| Pavlovian response |
mynd i lawr
rainpooled eyes
downhill &:

drOp

Monocoque/ 6061-T6 OS Reynolds Custom
                        Butted Aluminium Tube
                            Fox 32 Float Performance
                        RL FIT 140 Tapered 15QR
rear   sh o ck: Fox   Evolution   RL

/ disc brake – release – disc BrAkE /
arms pumped like tyres

        & stAcked into treebark face-plant earsRinG
                            << Blugrass FullFaceHelmet
                (I like my   t e e t h)

& find time [inside the rain] beyond thought this is my church
this is alive this is freedom from the mind & the only voice is the
forest's she knows who I am

        at home skeleton trees are seared inside eyelids

                                my name is Sophie
        it's been one week//two yyyears – no — thrEE hOurs
                                since my last {ride}

swim (Llyn Tegid)

November water fractures into face
slate-lakes the mind
wiped clean I cannot remember how
    to breathe in and judder
      like the death of a car pushed
       quietly over the edge
        swallowed by brackish
          water & fishmouthed

            I mimic exhaling hear nothing
             but the voice of the lake

               as she hums

               arms stretch, pull, knees in, twist out
            around & kick frog-like through
       viscous water now bubblemouthed
     I murmur leaves into poems
fold time-lapsed
    hands

     & sink.

murmuration

We barricade
      our hearts
        against
the setting sun.

                     Like h^{u}r^{r}i^{c}a^{n}e^{d}
                         s.a.n...ds shift[ing]

            &csiffts like *awen*
        Then Clou?.ds &
            like (not)-knowing,,,

     into red||||sunset
          black dye {{seeps
       acrossautumn s k y –
A geniiii escApes.

in situ

we are now accepting applications for our next writer in residence. the successful candidate must be able to demonstrate the ability to interact with the surrounding environment and create art from this experience in a meaningful way that will inspire future residencies.

a strong collaborative approach is required as well as the capacity to understand working as part of a whole. your thoughts will not be attributed to you. understand that these are not your ideas.

all of this existed before you, and will continue after you die. what you produce belongs here (you do not live, or create, in a vacuum).

take off your shoes. abandon the ego. all poetry, prose, blogs, essays or non-fiction-prose written during these residencies will be credited to 'Anon' and disseminated for free without your permission or knowledge.

you own creation no more than the air filling your lungs.

you could try to control it. breathe it in. hold on to it. charge us to share it. let us know how you get on with that.

in the meantime – residency applications are accepted on a rolling basis. each judged solely on artistic merit and the candidate's ability to engage with the principles above.

your successes may not be regarded as such by the wider artistic community for some time. or until after your death. or ever. additionally a number of artists will claim their residencies to be the most artistically valid. this may only be proved false some time after their death. and yours.

we do not yet have the systems in place to amend this unfortunate anomaly. however, you determine the length of your residency. while here all of your needs will be taken care of. shelter wherever feels comfortable. eat and drink whatever you find. it is important to note that no additional stipend is available.

we eagerly anticipate your application and look forward to collaborating with you in the future.

The Remembering

You are stacked like mountain strata; the sun bakes you. Carved from rock, you are a brick in the building of this community. The winds of change are a thousand sledgehammers pummelling walls, smashing slates from the roof that clatter to the floor with the sound of galloping horses.

The keys you are handed are silver fish that shimmer through grasping fingers. You reach for buckets to catch them but the buckets are seals streamlining along pews, gobbling the diaspora.

Dŵr dach chi. Pysgodyn dach chi. Morloi dach chi.

You are the weight of stories pinning walls to the ground – somebody needs to do something before the building is washed away with the morning birdsong. You determine that the Ghost Ship Tabernacle will sail long after the great desert dunes have swallowed Llandudno whole and weave your song into her.

Mae'r iaith Gymraeg wedi bod yr adeiladwr, y friciau, a'r gerdd.

Scrabbling in the sand you realise you cannot root. You try to dig but your hands are nets, your fingers are knots. Your heart is an anchor. You are weighted down by the debris washing from the building – each slate and brick you snag is a small history being eroded into sand and you cannot let them go.

Turning to the pulpit, you pray and wait to hear voices. Out of The Great Silence appear words. Your eyes are sealed shut like church windows but your mind is a projector of past and future and you witness Lewis Valentine speak hurricanes. His words are storms. *Mae o'n siarad cymylau. Mae o'n siarad dân.*

He speaks of a world of which you know nothing, and everything. His words fall like raindrops – *mae hi'n bwrw hen wragedd a ffyn* and those complaining of getting soaked are wearing the wrong clothes. As you listen, ropy fingers begin to unknot. Veins and arms and legs fray into roots that burrow through sand. You look around to see other people also rooting – becoming The Remembering. Your back, that had been stooped for so long, now stretches to the sky along with your neighbours'. *Cefn morfil dach chi.*

You forest together. Weave branches. Root *hanes*. Each future event is a leaf unfurling. Sprouting from your hands, your arms, your neighbour's legs, they whip like birds' wings – beat the future into being.

The pulpit is a pod of dolphins. The Tabernacle's walls are your forest. The roof is a flock of seagulls rising in prayer to Valentine's bright sun.

Hanes dach chi. Dysgu dach chi. Dyfodol dach chi.

From the Ashes

The Albatross straps a leather sack of infinite ideas
across her feathered breast and, rising
to greet the sun, locks wings out.

In the cold blue sky
white clouds wrap her in myth.
When she settles her feathers are
plucked by people who have lost all sense of their own worth.

One final sharp tug and the bird is bald
grounded like the rest of us.
The oven lit for supper.

She is ugly and ungainly, her flesh
tough and chewy, we wail
while threading feathers and curiosities
from the sack onto fat necklaces.

That night our eyes billow with clouds,
white bellies distend like volcanoes
belching white-hot fire
and curses.

The next morning, mourning over
the newly barren ground,
we scatter on the wind to salve burned skin
with patterns of stars seared into our eyes.

She was difficult to stomach –

the starling risen from the ashes.

Methuselah

I am in no rush
to grow tall or wise
or to be great
the yellow sun continues to shine
over black clouds
winter gives herselff over to spring
      so that I do not need to hurry one green
      leaff
                            away

I will gnarl here
ffold time into skin
experience into time
root with ageing ffingers
into landscape/into selff

I am not of the straight & true
sometimes my ffruit is small and bitter
the fflesh hard
skin thickened

Limbs twisting like coiled snakes
I wail with
bird & shadow
with rat & earth

Holding each moment
precious:
tremulous or unwavering

    these experiences shape me
like a riverbank
        or song

Dharma

Lines written on the overnight train from Varanasi to Kolkata

The Prophets of the past have nothing left
to teach you, no time has ever existed like this
that they could have foreseen. The Great Wheel
is turning and you will change with it
or you will not.

We reach down into earth to embrace
the darkness in each other. The last great poem
has already been written and will continue
to write itself until you accept you are the author
and the only way of concluding is to search
deep inside yourself for the beginning.

You hold the answers to everything.
You are the universe in flesh and water.
There is nothing you don't already know.
Learn to hear your truth.
Understand what it is you are given.
Your mind speaks to you.
Listen.

Rediscover yourself slowly,
over decades, like reincarnated lovers.

Create in order to radically transform
your life, not to satisfy the intellectual curiosity
of yourself, or others.

This path begins with horror at the strange,
the familiar eventually terrifies.
You fear not only yourself, but them:
know that your community are not your enemy.
Know that your enemy is not your enemy.
A forest only causes you to walk miles in the wrong direction
if you didn't bother to map her soul.
You are afraid and lazy and as such will work diligently
– long hours into the night – to avoid facing the unease,
the awkwardness, the sense of utter failure.
Do not shy from this truth – the world will continue
to make life difficult until you stop choosing
the easy path every time.

Your inner landscape houses the ghosts you feed
are you still pretending they are not real?
These are the dead spirits of all the promises you made
and didn't keep. Know that your heart beat stronger making
them
and crumbled realising the lie.

You have shored the broken pottery of your heart
against the ocean of time and we are riding a great wave
into the unknown. Accept that everything is known
until this point – all of time exists as one – but we are
reaching
A Great Ending or Great Beginning and you cannot change
anything
except yourself. If you are the one thing you think is right
with the world then you are the problem.

Do not believe what I say.
You know your truth, it is a pack of hungry wolves
tracking you across the frozen tundra of your emotional life.
Once they have devoured you the crows will amass
to pick over the carcass of your ignorance.
You will be scattered in their shit across the face of the earth,
perhaps then you will understand how much you have been
loved.

Until this time seek truths
know that every answer you hunt is an animal
stealth-stepping through the landscape of your mind.
It is for you to seek out and understand the way of the hunter
the way of crow and kite
the last blue whale.
You do this by connecting with the external:
when did you last swim in the ocean?
Or murmurate like starlings?
Or wake at dawn to praise the sun?
When did you last unravel the knots in your intestines
by feeding only on the emotions your stomach needs?
Do you know what you need?

Try this:
Live as closely to nature as possible.
Create. Love.

Everything else is superfluous.
Everything else is part of the lie that keeps you
enslaved like a battery hen when the door is open.

Your body knows what you need and
you can either lift your face up to the heavens
and give thanks to the soft rain praising your skin
or you can hide in brick houses, behind solid doors
that ostracise the sun and moon and feed the whispers
in your lungs telling you the problem is with other people.

Do not lose yourself in dreams of shaping cities
in your own image, stay away from anything that reassures
you
the world needs your meddling.

Your alien heart will still beat
and deep within you the mountain echoes.
If you cannot hear this
you must stop everything until you can.
Or continue as you are, until you can.
It is all the same.

The Great Wheel is turning and you will change with it
Or you will not.

Acknowledgements

Rebel Sun: published in *Dark Mountain* anthology 11, spring 2017.

My Mother Speaks Thorns: *Picaroon Poetry*, March 2017.

Waiting for Awen, Dharma and **cumulonimbus:** written as part of the Artist in Residence programme for *Wales Arts Review*, January 2017.

Dharma: also written as part of the Wales/India project supporter by *Parthian Books, Literature Wales, British Council Wales* and *Wales Arts International.*

The disappearing (a manifesto): published in the *Caught by the River Antidote to Indifference* magazine December 2016.

Eleven signs you are escaping insanity: published in *Bare Fiction* magazine, issue 8, Aug 2016.

Cymro: commissioned by the *Wales Millennium Centre* for the Aberfan Memorial Concert held on 8th October 2016 and published in the programme. Performed by *Michael Sheen* OBE.

Paper News: performed at *Penguin Random House*, Strand, London on Monday 3rd October for the Young People's Laureate London announcement.

My mother speaks thorns, Iron will, Bearhug, Reincarnation (or the visualisation of patriarchy) and Elemental all began life during a week-long writing retreat July 2016, at Tŷ Newydd headed by Pascale Petit and Pamela Robertson-Pearce.

Sale and InsOmnia: both published in the autumn 2016 issue of *The Lonely Crowd*. InsOmnia also first written and performed for *VoiceBox Insomnia Revolutions* event at *UnDegUn Arts Space*, summer 2016.

Process (in memory): won the *Out Spoken* award for Innovation in Poetry 2015.

Follow the White Dog, Conservation and Community Artistry: versions of these were published in issue 2 of the online poetry magazine *The Curly Mind*.

Topography (plygu): published in autumn 2016 issues of *Poetry Wales*.

The Remembering: Commissioned by *Culture Action Llandudno* for the Tabernacle Sunday Service, Llandudno. Sunday 27th November 2016.

Notes

the disappearing (a manifesto): Best to be like water - the *Tao Te Ching*. Translated by Stephen Addiss and Stanley Lombardo

Eleven Signs you are Escaping Insanity: *Mae gynnoch chi ymwybyddiaeth mewn amgylchedd. Mae eich mynyddoedd chi'n lonydd* [Cymraeg] You have an awareness of the environment. Your mountains are tranquil.

Y Niwl [Cymraeg]: The Fog.

Elemental: Anne Waldman is the author of more than 40 collections of poetry and poetics. She is an active member of the Outrider experimental poetry movement, and has been connected to the Beat movement and the second generation of the New York School – Poetry Foundation.

Cosmic Satnav: with thanks to Jodie Ashdown for this title.

Cymro [Cymraeg]: Brother.

Waiting for Awen: *Awen* [Cymraeg] Muse or inspiration.

Community Artistry: *Sut dach chi'n gweu efo'ch gilydd?* [Cymraeg] How do we knit together?

Our histories have deserted us: poem inspired by the Greek proverb: *Ουδέν μονιμότερον του προσωρινού* – The only permanence is change, possibly from the philosopher Heraclitus.

Collector of Songs: *yn Saesneg* [Cymraeg] in English.

Expectation: *neu addo a bygwth* [Cymraeg] or promises and threats.
bydd hi'n ddiwrnod ansefydlog yfory gwasgedd isel / yn dod â gwyntoedd cryfion a glaw}}} [Cymraeg] tomorrow will be unsettled with low pressure bringing strong winds and rain. Taken from a BBC weather report.

Process (in memory): *roedd o'n dydd Iau yn Gymru* [Cymraeg] it was a Thursday in Wales.
'가만히 있으라' [Korean] stay there.
바다 속에서 헤엄치는 꿈을 일주일 내내 꾸었습니다 [Korean] I had a dream of swimming in the sea all week, Eunjin Choi.

Silver Fish: written the day after Trump's election.

topography (plygu): in Welsh *plygu* means 'to fold', *mewnblyg* means 'introverted', literally 'to fold in', and *allblyg* means extroverted 'to fold out'.
Terra nullius [Latin] Nobody's land.
Mynyddoedd [Cymraeg] Mountains.

conservation: a poem written splicing text from various news articles, blogs and websites about hunting and war.

Inside Goldstein's Mind: Leonard Goldstein was a Marxist scholar. Hounded out of various university posts in America because of his politics during the McCarthy era, he settled in East Berlin. The library amassed over his lifetime was donated to Glyndwr University, Wrexham in 2011 just before Leonard's death in order to fulfill his wishes that the library of over 13,000 books remain as a complete collection and resource for students. Goldstein would often write his thoughts onto tracing paper and glue them into the books – the ephemera of bookmarks, notes and postcards is as interesting as the books themselves. At this time of writing there isn't enough funding to open the library and the doors remain closed.

flo: Inspired by a series of writing residencies undertaken in care homes across *Y Gogledd Cymru* / North Wales for Age Cymru.

swim: *Llyn Tegid* [Cymraeg] Bala Lake.

The Remembering: Lewis Valentine was one of the original founders of Plaid Cymru who became an activist after the British government established a bombing school at Penyberth on the *Llŷn* peninsula. Along with Saunders Lewis and DJ Williams, Valentine spent nine months imprisoned in Wormwood Scrubs for protesting and on release they were greeted as heroes.
Dŵr dach chi. Pysgodyn dach chi. Morloi dach chi. [Cymraeg] You are water. You are fish. You are seals.
Mae'r iaith Gymraeg wedi bod yr adeiladwr, y friciau, a'r gerdd.

[Cymraeg] The Welsh language has been the builder, the bricks and the poem.

Mae o'n siarad cymylau. Mae o'n siarad dân. [Cymraeg] He speaks clouds. He speaks fire.

mae hi'n bwrw hen wragedd a ffyn [Cymraeg] an old Welsh idiom: it's raining old ladies and sticks.

Cefn morfil dach chi. [Cymraeg] You are a whale's back.

Hanes dach chi. Dysgu dach chi. Dyfodol dach chi. [Cymraeg] You are the history/story. You are learning/teaching. You are the future.

Methuselah: the man reported to have lived the longest (969) in the Hebrew Bible.

ff is one letter in Cymraeg and is pronounced like the English f.